You don't raise heroes; you raise sons.
And if you treat them like sons,
they'll turn out to be heroes,
even if it's just in your own eyes.

WALTER SCHIRRA, SR.

Mother Remembers

For My Son

EDITED BY CASSANDRA CASE

DESIGNED BY FABIA WARGIN DESIGN

STERLING PUBLISHING CO., INC.

The present is the living sum-total of the whole past.

THOMAS CARLYLE

Published by Sterling Publishing Company, Inc.
387 Park Avenue South, New York, NY 10016
Printed in China

STERLING ISBN 0-8069-9147-X

Gathered together for:

Noah Michael Anderson

Memory is history recorded in our brain,
memory is a painter,
it paints pictures of the past and of the day.

GRANDMA MOSES

With love from:

Mom

Contents

Dear Son, This is for you, because...

Keep some souvenirs of your past,
or how will you ever prove
it wasn't all a dream?

ASHLEIGH BRILLIANT

About Your Mother...Me

My given names . . . .

. . . .

My nicknames . . . .

. . . .

Date of my birth . . . .

. . . .

Place of my birth . . . .

. . . .

When I was born I was so surprised
I didn't talk for a year and a half.

GRACIE ALLEN

Pictures of Me

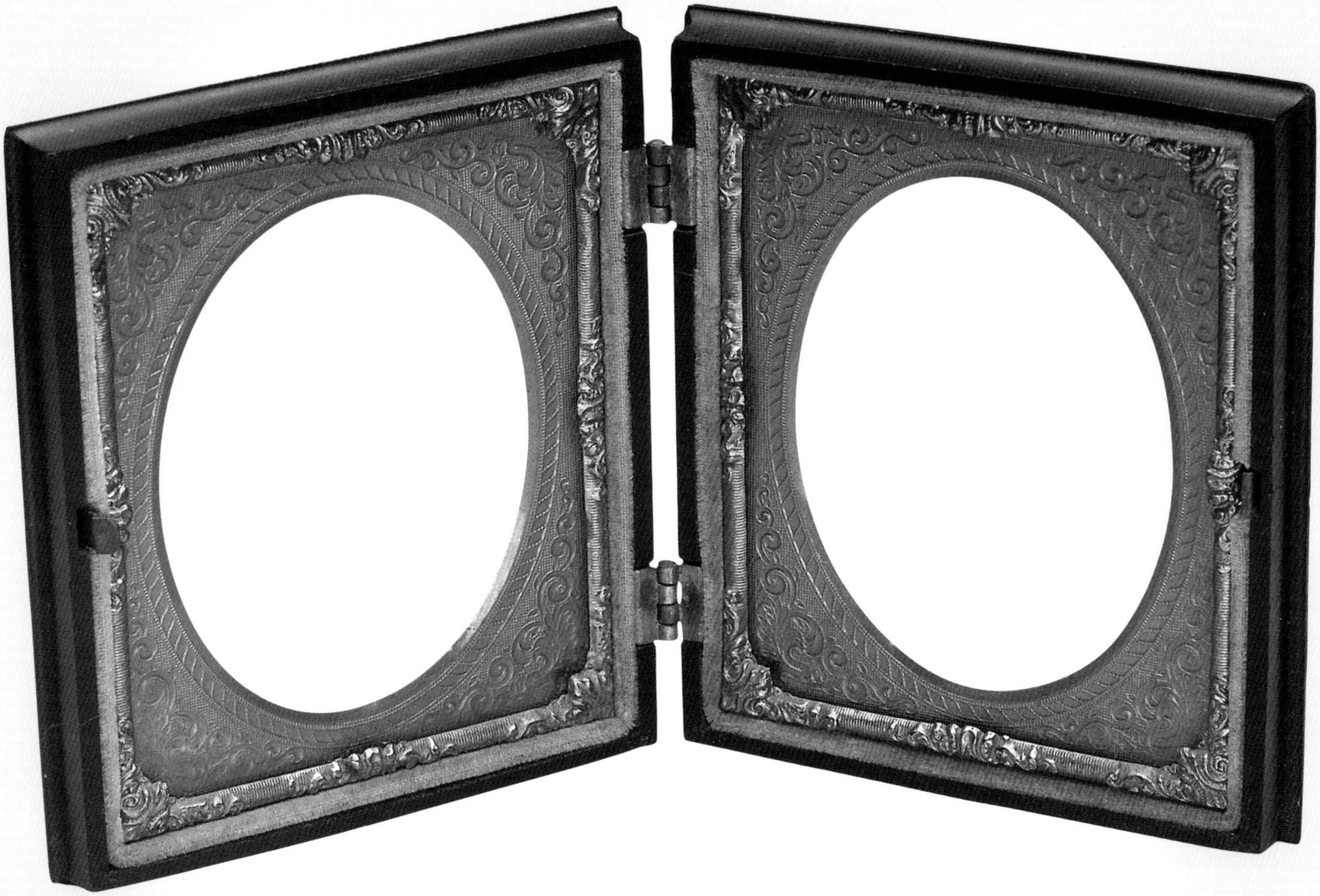

I Remember My Mother and Father

(your grandmother and grandfather)

What you called your grandmother and grandfather

What I Remember About My Grandparents

(your great grandparents) and other people who cared for me when I was little

The simplest toy, one that even the youngest child can operate, is called a grandparent.

SAM LEVENSON

When I Was Little

My earliest memories

My favorite memories

The spirit of a three-year-old lasts a hundred years.

JAPANESE PROVERB

My favorite toys

Pictures of My Family

The Place Where I Grew Up

. . . .

. . . .

Home is not a structure, but something in your heart.

AMERICAN PROVERB

What We Did in Summer

Kids I Played With

Their names and who they were to me

Our favorite things to do

You can discover more about a person in an hour of play than in a year of conversation.

PLATO

Games We Liked

Indoor games

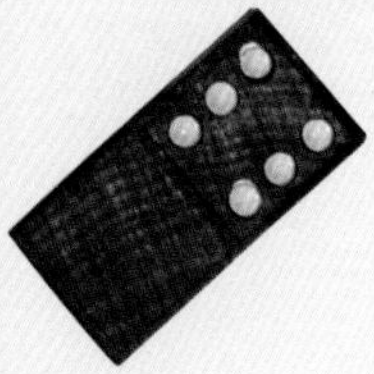

Outdoor games and sports

Make-believe

Pets I Had

Pets' names . . . .

. . . .

. . . .

Pets I Wanted

Reasons I couldn't have them

Off to School

Schools I went to

How I got to school

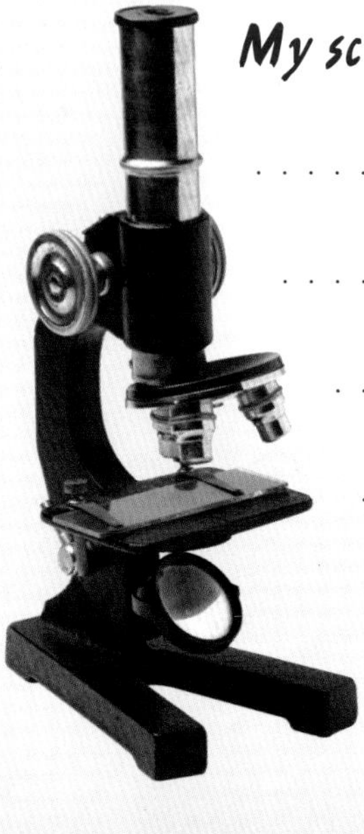

My school friends

Memorable teachers

Me as a Teenager

My room

My girlfriends

My boyfriends

(or boys I had a crush on)

What We Thought Was "In"

The music we listened to

Styles we liked to wear

Cars we drove

Entertainment

Firsts and Funnies

First job

First car

First love

First time on my own

Funny stories

What I Did When I Finished High School

Where I went

Special things I did

Some of My Favorite People

Favorite Times in My Life

How I Met Your Father

What it was that I liked about him

Places we went together

How he proposed

Your Maternal Family Tree

YOUR MOTHER

....
Name

....
Date of birth

....
Place of birth

YOUR GRANDMOTHER

....
Name

....
Date of birth

....
Place of birth

YOUR GRANDFATHER

....
Name

....
Date of birth

....
Place of birth

Your grandmother's Mother

....

....

Your grandmother's Father

....

....

Your grandfather's Mother

....

....

Your grandfather's Father

....

....

Your grandmother's Grandmother

....

....

Your grandmother's Grandfather

....

....

Your grandfather's Grandmother

....

....

Your grandfather's Grandfather

....

....

Your Paternal Family Tree

YOUR FATHER

....
Name

....
Date of birth

....
Place of birth

YOUR GRANDMOTHER

....
Name

....
Date of birth

....
Place of birth

YOUR GRANDFATHER

....
Name

....
Date of birth

....
Place of birth

Your grandmother's Mother

....

....

Your grandmother's Father

....

....

Your grandfather's Mother

....

....

Your grandfather's Father

....

....

Your grandmother's Grandmother

....

....

Your grandmother's Grandfather

....

....

Your grandfather's Grandmother

....

....

Your grandfather's Grandfather

....

....

Our Wedding

The day . . . .

The time . . . .

The place . . . .

The party we had

Where we went for our honeymoon

When I Knew You Were on the Way

How I felt

. . . .

Whom we told first

. . . .

I begin to love this little creature,
and to anticipate his birth as a fresh twist to a knot,
which I do not wish to untie.

MARY WOLLSTONECRAFT SHELLEY

When You Were Born

Date . . . .

Time . . . .

Place . . . .

Your weight and length . . . .

My lovely living boy,
My hope, my hap, my love,
My life, my joy.

GUILLAUME DE SALLUSTE
SEIGNEUR DU BARTES

You!

Your name . . . .

The meaning of your name . . . .

. . . .

. . . .

How we decided on your name . . . .

. . . .

. . . .

Other names we thought about . . . .

. . . .

. . . .

Compliments you received

. . . .

. . . .

. . . .

. . . .

. . . .

Gifts you received

. . . .

. . . .

. . . .

. . . .

. . . .

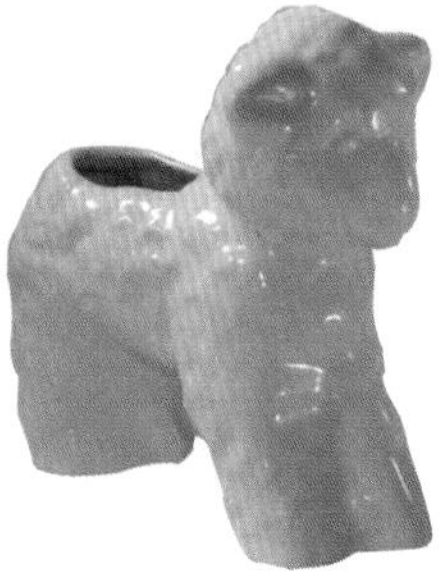

When We Brought You Home

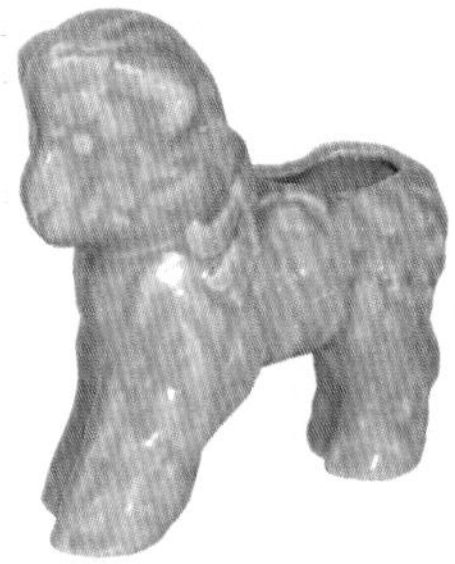

Your first days in the family

There is nothing more thrilling in this world,
I think, than having a child that is yours,
and yet is mysteriously a stranger.

AGATHA CHRISTIE

More Photos of You!

Babies are such a nice way to start people.

DAN HERALD

Things I Wanted to Tell You

How I felt

What your father did

Things you did

There is nothing more absorbing than a baby,
nothing more intoxicating.

MARY GORDON

Memorable Moments

When you first smiled . . . .

. . . .

When you first rolled over by yourself . . . .

. . . .

Your first solid food . . . .

. . . .

Your favorite foods . . . .

. . . .

When you first stood up . . . .

. . . .

Your first birthday party . . . .

. . . .

When you first walked by yourself . . . .

. . . .

Your first words . . . .

. . . .

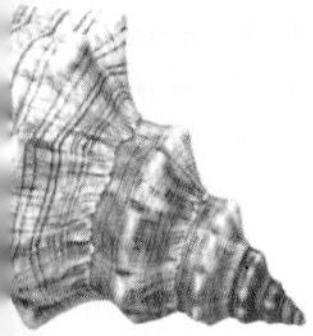

Sleepytime

Bedtime rituals . . . .

When you woke up at night . . . .

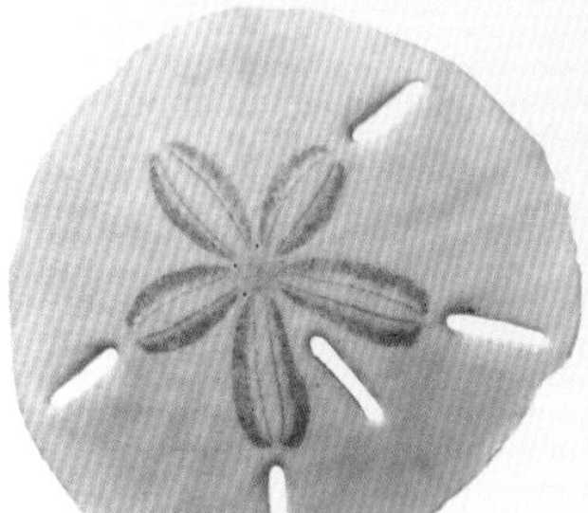

I love the child just
Falling asleep;
Give him a golden dream
To keep!

MARCELINE DESBORDES-VALMORE

Music

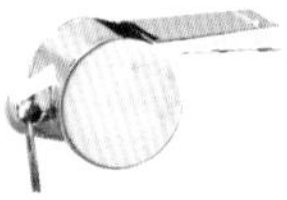

First songs you liked me to sing

First songs you sang

Music you responded to

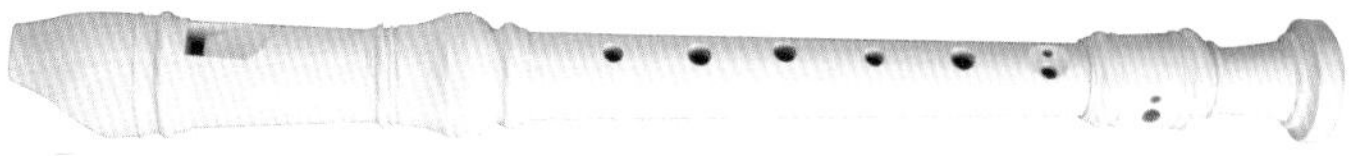

How you responded

Over in the meadow
In a hole in a tree
Lived an old mother bluebird
And her little birdies three.
"Sing!" said the mother;
"We sing!" said the three.
So they sang and were glad
In a hole in the tree.

OLIVE A. WADSWORTH

Books, Toys and TV

Favorite books

Favorite TV programs and videos

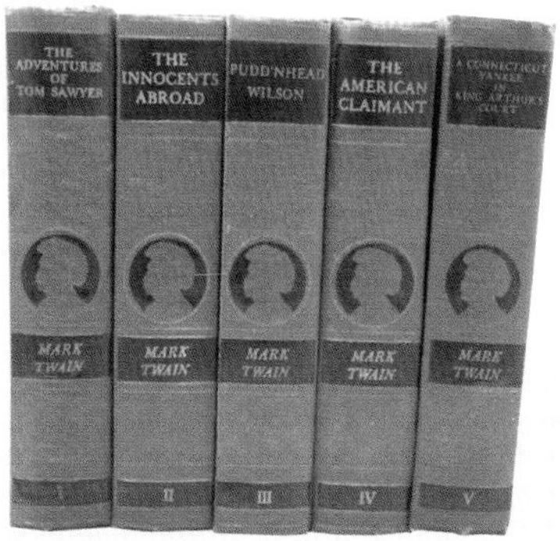

There is no frigate
like a book
to take us lands away.

EMILY DICKINSON

Favorite toys

There, in the night, where none can spy
All in my hunter's camp I lie,
And play at books that I have read
Till it is time to go to bed.

ROBERT LOUIS STEVENSON

Growing Up ...

Seeing you sleeping peacefully on your back among your stuffed ducks, bears and basset hounds would remind me that no matter how good the next day might be, certain moments were gone forever.

JOAN BAEZ

Favorite Games, Indoors and Out

Whom you played with

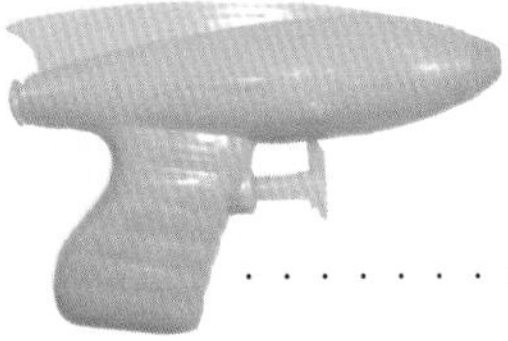

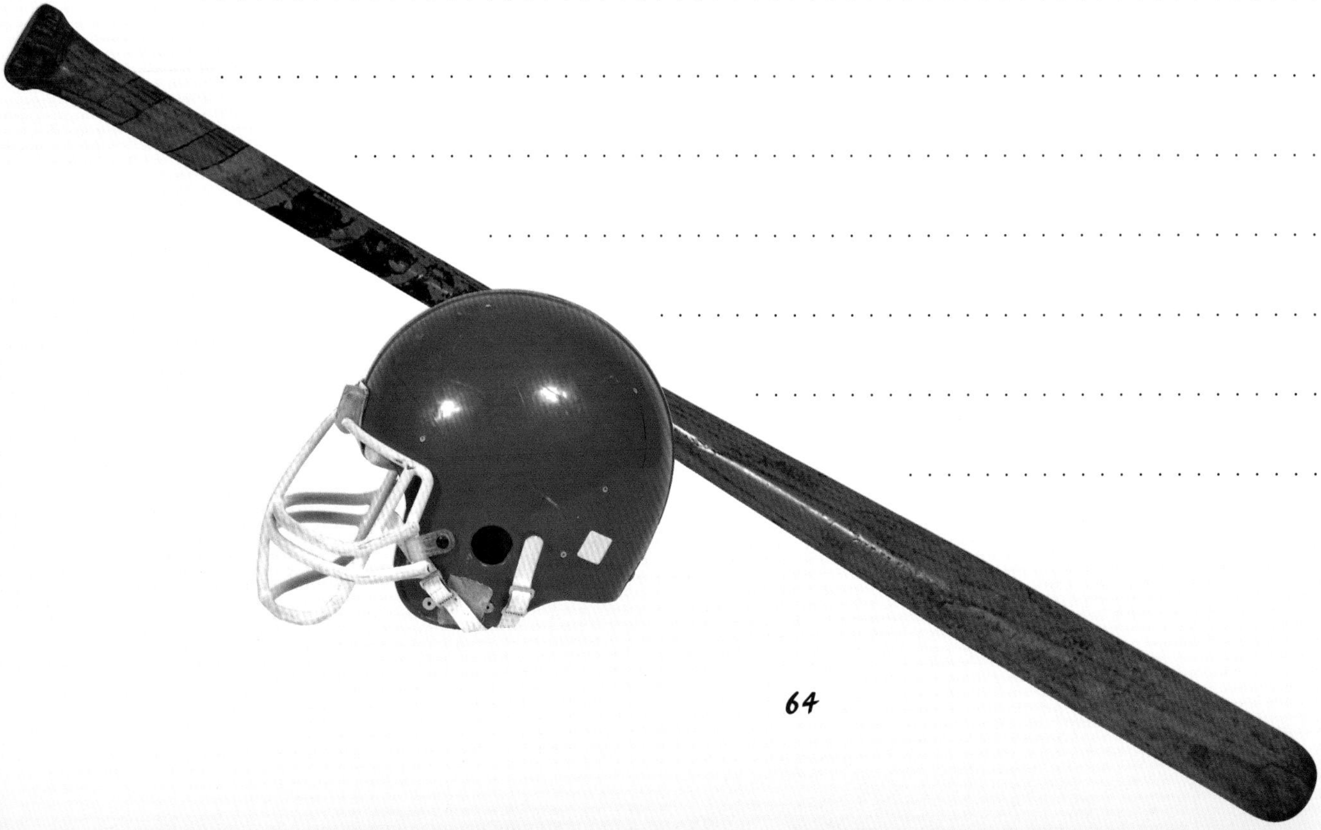

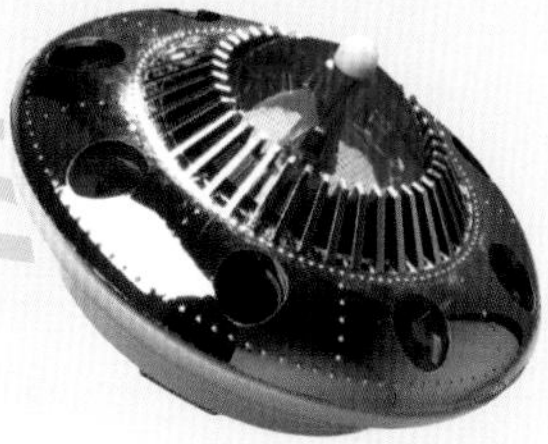

School

Your first day at school

New friends

Favorite teachers

After school activities

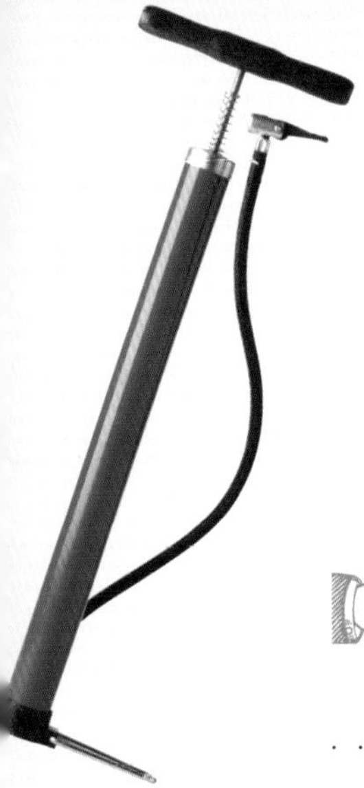

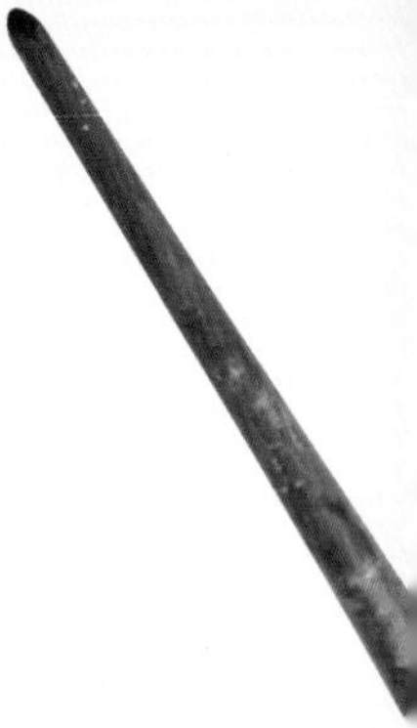

Stages and Milestones

Things you did

Things you said

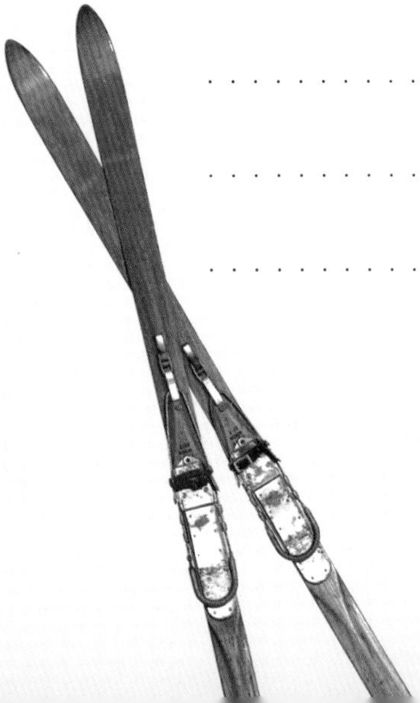

Some thoughts and feelings I had

Things We Did Together

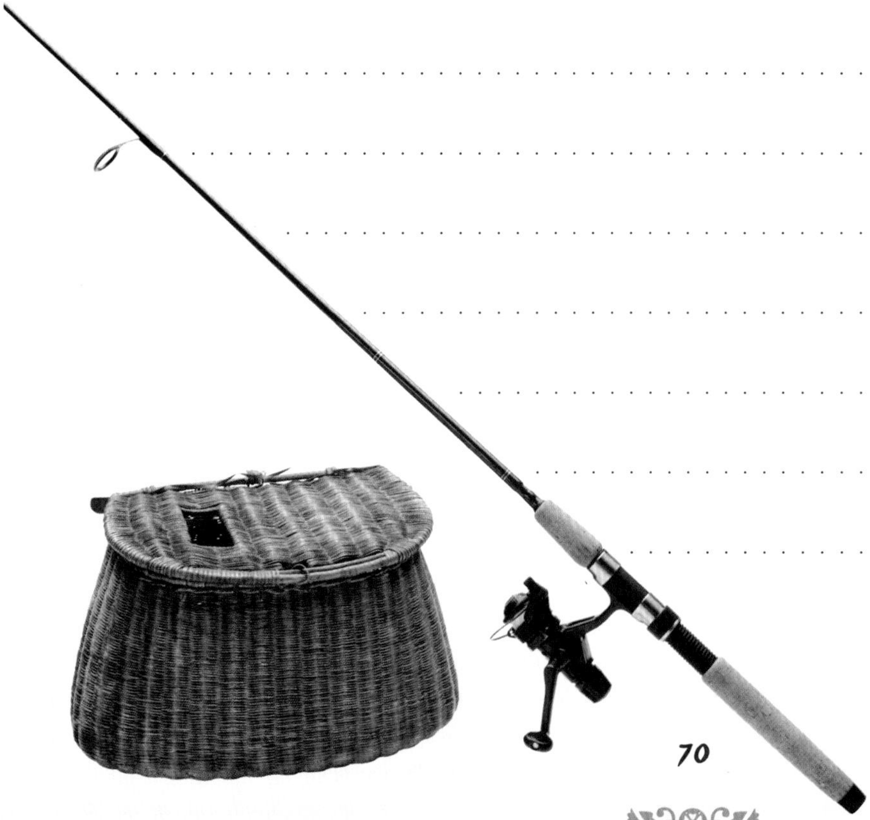

That is the best – to laugh with someone
because you both think the same things are funny.

GLORIA VANDERBILT

Places We Went

Be careful going in search of adventure –
it's ridiculously easy to find.

WILLIAM LEAST HEAT MOON

Clippings, Souvenirs and Mementos

B I N G
12 18
My Scrap Book

Thoughts to Hold on To

Always dream and shoot higher than you know you can do.

WILLIAM FAULKNER

You will do foolish things, but do them with enthusiasm.

COLETTE

Fall seven times, stand up eight.

JAPANESE PROVERB

Change is always powerful. Let your hook be always cast.
In the pool where you least expect it, will be a fish.

OVID

Hopes, Wishes and Prayers for You, My Son

No one knows what it is that he can do until he tries.

PUBLILIUS SYRUS

Him that I love, I wish to be free – even from me.

ANNE MORROW LINDBERGH